The Space Within...

Talks on Meditation by

H. H. SRI SRI RAVI SHANKAR

THE SPACE WITHIN...

Printed in India by Jwalamukhi Job Press, Bangalore
Ph.: +91-80-26601064, 26608090

Edited in 2006:   Puravi Hegde
Designed in 2006: Debbie Swart

ISBN 978-81-907964-5-3

Published by:
Sri Sri Publications Trust,
21ˢᵗ km, Kanakapura Road, Udaypura,
Bangalore – 560082, Phone: 080 32722473
email: info@srisripublications.com
www.artoflivingshop.com

CONTENTS

PREFACE

One of the world's most inspirational and dynamic leaders, His Holiness Sri Sri Ravi Shankar, is also one of the most original thinkers of our times. Emphasising practical wisdom, he has transformed millions of lives all over the globe. His talks are a unique blend of knowledge and guidance, delivered with simplicity and humour – a powerful, unbeatable combination that touches lives and hearts, wherever heard.

It is with great joy that we offer this special package that includes a truly spectacular collection of talks on meditation, given by His Holiness Sri Sri Ravi Shankar, over a period of time, and a CD, wherein His Holiness, Himself, lovingly guides you through a unique meditation... to the tranquil space within.

MEDITATION: A TRIP TO NOWHERE

At the top of the world, there is nowhere to go. Nowhere is really "now here", and whenever and wherever you are, you are nowhere!

Whenever you are nowhere, you can't but be on top of the world! So make everywhere and all time nowhere.

You have to pierce through nowhere... and find you are Now Here.

Here, at the top of the world, not just the depth of the ocean is still – even the waves are frozen. Like the mind in meditation – cool and still; but for a gentle breeze, like the tiny breath – all is still.

Stillness is the purest form of awareness that is present before birth and after death.

Wisdom is to recognize the stillness amidst activity. The repeated experience of meditation helps you to "live the stillness", even amidst chaos.

(A Drop of Knowledge from the North Pole)

DEMYSTIFYING MEDITATION

What is meditation?

A mind without agitation...
is meditation.

A mind in the present moment...
is meditation.

A mind, which becomes "no mind"...
is meditation.

A mind that has no hesitation, no anticipation...
is meditation.

A mind that has come back home, to the source...
is meditation.

When can you rest? When is rest possible?

Rest is *only* possible, when you have *stopped* all other activities – isn't it? When you stop moving around, when you stop working, thinking, talking, seeing, hearing, smelling, tasting... – when all these activities stop – then you get rest. When you stop all *voluntary* activities, then, you rest. When all voluntary activities are arrested, or stopped, and you are left with just the involuntary activities (breathing, beating of the heart, digestion of food by the stomach, blood circulation, etc.) – this is sleep; this is rest – but, this is *not* total rest.

See from your own experience. You go to bed with some restlessness, agitation, or desire... and you cannot sleep deeply. The mind is planning, and planning, and planning... and when you go to sleep, those plans are still in the mind, those ambitions are still there. They go a little deeper, and so at the surface level, for a little while, they seem to not be there, but when we have a lot of ambitions, or desires, our sleep is not very deep. So very ambitious people cannot sleep deeply because inside, their minds are not hollow and empty – the mind is not free. When the *mind* settles down, then *total re5t* happens – *meditation* happens.

What does "focus" mean?

Focus is being fulfilled in the moment, being centred. It is looking to the highest, and remaining in that space of peace. No peace means – no focus. When you are at peace, focus is already happening. Similarly, if you focus, you attain peace. If you are not focussed, your mind hovers around, and there is no peace.

Look into your own life… You are bothered, if you *have* things, and you are bothered, if you *don't have* things! Do you see what I am saying? You have a companion – that is a botheration; if you don't have a companion – that is *also* a botheration. If you have money – that is a botheration. If you don't have money, even then, you are bothered! If you have money, you are afraid, or worried, and you are always thinking about what to do with this money: "What do I do? Should I invest it, or not?" If you invest, you are worried about whether the money is growing, or reducing, or you are anxious about what is happening in the share market – the fluctuations in the share market. However, even if you don't want to invest, then also there is botheration!

Liberation is total freedom – you are not bothered, when things are there… and you are not bothered, even if they are not there.

Real freedom is freedom from the future and freedom from the past. When you are not happy in the present moment, then you desire a bright future. Desire *means* the present moment is not all right! It causes tension in the mind. Every desire causes feverishness… and then, in this state, meditation is far away from happening. You may sit with your eyes closed, but desires keep arising, thoughts keep arising – and you fool yourself that you are meditating, when actually, you are daydreaming!

Meditation is accepting this moment – living every moment *totally*, with depth.

If and when desires come up, you "offer them away", that is meditation – not holding on to them. You have no control over desires. Even if you say, "I shouldn't be desirous," that is another desire!

"Oh! I should not desire. Desire is a cause of misery. I shouldn't have desires. When will I be free of desires?" is another desire! As desires come up, recognize them, and let go. This process is called "*sanyasa*". Offer all desires, as they come, as they rise in you... and be centred. When you are able to do this – when you are in your centre – then, *nothing* can shake you; *nothing* can take you away from this – otherwise, some small thing can shake you, and then you are sad, or upset.

What are you upset over? A few words, from here, or there? A few words can make you sad: "Oh! I am in *this* group, I am in *that* group. Why should *I* not be there? I *should* have been there. Is this a *test* for me?"

How easily can you let go of all this?

That is the "art of letting go". Life teaches you the art of letting go at *every* event, in *every* event, and the more you learn to let go, the happier and freer you are! Otherwise, you carry the *same* world with you: "Oh! The Guru looked at me! He didn't talk to me... He didn't see me..." – then, *where* is the mind meditating?! What is the use?! How does it matter, whether the Master looks at you, or not? Let go!

When you learn to let go, you will be joyful... and as you start being joyful, *more* will be given to you. Those, who have, will be given more – *that* is meditation.

As long as some desires linger in your mind, your mind *cannot* be at total rest. Take a good look at the desires – "*What* is this desire? This is a *futile* thing, a *small* desire. What I'm 'having' is nothing much. There's nothing big in it; nothing great." This is maturity. This is called *discrimination*. Discrimination is saying, "This is all nothing. So what?!" Taking a good look at one's desires, and realising that they are futile or nothing great, is maturity or discrimination.

The other way, is to extend your desire – Make it so big! Then too, it won't bother you. It is the tiny sand particle that irritates your eye – a big stone, a rock, can never get into your eye; it cannot irritate you!

As long as some desires linger in your mind, you *cannot* be in total rest. In the Bhagawad Gita, Lord Krishna says, "You cannot get into *yoga* (union with Self), unless you drop the desires and hankerings in you."

As long as you hold on to "doing" something (doer-ship), as long as you hold on to some planning ("I want to do this, I want to do this…"), your mind does not settle. Every desire, or ambition, is like a sand particle in one's eyes – they irritate. You cannot shut your eyes, nor keep them open, if there's a particle of sand inside your eyes – it's uncomfortable either way. Dispassion is removing this particle of dust, or sand, from your eye, so that you can open and shut your eyes freely – you can enjoy the world freely, you can relax, and get relief from it, freely.

Nahya sanyasta sankalpo, yogi bhavati kashchana

Do you see the mechanics? Once again, go by your own experience – When you want to sleep, just before you sleep, if you plan, "Oh! I must do this! Oh! I must do this!" – do you enjoy a good sleep? The more anxious you are about doing something, the more difficult it becomes to sleep. What do you do, before going to bed, before going to sleep?

You simply let go of everything! Only if you simply let go of everything, before falling asleep, will you be able to rest.

Why not do the same thing with respect to activity, moment by moment? Atleast, when you want to sit for meditation, or during meditation, let go of everything. The best way to do this is to think or feel: "The world is disappearing, dissolving, dead... I am dead!"

Unless you are dead, you cannot meditate!!!

For many, the mind doesn't even settle after death! Wise are those, whose minds can settle, when they are alive.

What is it that you can *hold* on to? You *cannot* even hold on to this *body* forever! Whatever care you take of it, one day it is still going to bid you goodbye! You will be forcefully evicted from this place; out of this world – with no prior notice! It will be immediate! There will be no time to pack your bags and baggage!

What is it that you are holding on to? What is it that you are looking for? Are you looking for some great joy? What great joy can come to you?? You *are joy*!

Have you seen dogs biting bones? Do you know *why* they bite bones?

While dogs bite and bite at bones... the hard bone makes wounds inside their mouths. The dog's own blood starts to ooze out, but the dog feels: "Oh! This bone is very tasty!" After a while, the dog's whole mouth gets swollen and sore. The poor dog spent so much time, chewing a bone... and getting nothing out of it! It didn't fill the dog's stomach, it didn't produce any juice... and yet the dog kept biting the bone, over and over, again and again.

Any joy you experience in life is from the depth – the depth of your Self. It's when you are able to let go of all that you are holding on to, and settle down, to being centred in that space. This act is called meditation. Actually, meditation is a "no act"! It is the art of non-doing – the art of doing nothing... and the rest in meditation is deeper than the deepest sleep that you can ever have! It is several times deeper, because in sleep, desires still linger on somewhere, but in meditation, you transcend all desires. This brings such coolness to the brain! It's like overhauling or servicing the whole body-mind complex.

Meditation is letting go of the anger from the past, letting go of the events of the past… and letting go of all planning for the future. Planning can hold you back from diving deep into yourself. Meditation, as I've said before, is accepting this moment, and living every moment totally, with depth.

Whatever you may plan, whatever you may do, your final destination is the grave! You live as a good man or a bad man, you cry or laugh – whatever you do – everybody goes to the grave. This is the *final* say! Have your sight on the final say. Before the body leaves you, *you* learn to leave everything. That is freedom.

Whether you are a sinner or a saint, you will be in a grave. Whether you are rich or poor, intelligent, dull, or a dumb fool, you will go to the grave. Whether you are loved or hated, you will be in a grave. Whether you love someone or hate anyone, you will go to the grave. People fought wars… and those, who lost, went to the grave… and those, who won, also went to the grave. What does it matter? It's just a matter of a few years – time gaps… Those, who lived, also suffered, and those who went, also went more peacefully.

So what are these little things that keep popping up in the mind, disallowing you to settle down and be at peace… be in joy… be in love?

Patients die... Doctors also die. They both go to the grave! Being a doctor doesn't mean one doesn't go to the grave, nor does it mean he (or she) keeps saving his (or her) patients all the time! It's an illusion!

It is said that God laughs on two occasions:
The first is when a doctor tells a patient, "Don't worry! *I* am here to save you!"

The second is when two people fight over a piece of land, saying, "This is *my* land!" or "That is *my* land!" Then God laughs: "You are both going to a grave, and yet you're saying 'This is *my* land, that is *your* land!'"

Dispassion can bring so much joy in your life. Don't think that dispassion is a state of apathy. There is a difference between dispassion and apathy.

"Oh! *Anyway* everybody is going to the grave… So what can one do now…" – This is apathy, not dispassion. There is incompleteness in the state of apathy.

Dispassion is full of enthusiasm and joy! It brings all the joy to your life… and it allows you to rest so well. When you rest well – when you go deep into meditation… and then come out of a deep meditation, you become very dynamic – you are able to act better. The deeper you are able to rest, the more dynamic you will be in activity. Even though deep rest and dynamic activity are opposite values, they are complementary.

Don't think that if you become dispassionate, you will renounce everything and run into a nunnery or monastery! Besides, people, who are in a nunnery or a monastery, are also daydreaming... daydreaming of heaven!

Once an old nun asked me, "Tell me, how is it in heaven? How is it there? I have no experience... (!) I am not used to new places. I am not used to sleeping in new places. I want to know so that I can get used to it!"
I said, "Don't worry! There, you will have a wonderful bed to sleep on. There will be several servants around you, to give you a massage and put you to rest!"

This doer-ship, this "planning", can hold you back from diving deep into your Self. Just your understanding that meditation is accepting this moment, and living every moment totally, with depth, is good enough. Let go... and see... Just this understanding, and a few days of the continuous practice of meditation can change the quality of our lives.

Do you see how very simple it is? It's not a serious thing at all!

THE ART OF LIVING

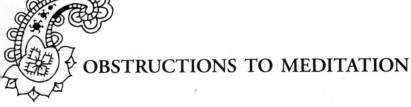

OBSTRUCTIONS TO MEDITATION

What obstructs meditation? What obstructs your silence?

It is desire and planning – It is your desire, your plans: "I want to do this... I want to do this... I want to do this..." – However, what happens is, you can't *quieten* your mind! You are sitting in meditation – you are meditating – but, what is happening?

Your desires keep bugging you... Your planning mind is busy planning... and all the plans will only "happen", when you sit for meditation! Yet, at the end, you will say, "I have meditated nicely... I have done my programme..."

What programme have you done?! *Where* did you do the programme?! Your mind is sitting there with your plans! Do you see that? You are planning with your eyes closed – you are dreaming with your eyes closed – Isn't it? And we think, "Oh! We have meditated for so many years!" – That is *no* meditation!

Your "plan" is a hindrance to meditation. So, how can you drop your planning?

One way to drop your planning is to *expand* your desire! After expanding your desire, "offer" it: "Okay! I offer this… Let it be done…" But the moment, you "offer" it, it becomes, "If it's right, it will be done for me," and *that* is called trust. It *will* happen! Just think it will happen… and you relax. Do you see, what I mean? This is called surrender.

Surrender means the ability to drop a desire, or a botheration, or something that keeps bugging us in the mind. "Okay, I'll drop it." – That is surrender. "If it is right for me, it will be done." Finished. Only then, is your mind, able to experience hollowness – that state of awareness.

Sometimes, when all your desires are fulfilled, or when that one desire that you were tied to in the mind, "sinks", then you say, "Oh! I had a wonderful meditation today!" This is because that day, you had the ability to drop your desires and plans… and relax. Hasn't this happened to everyone?

In the Bhagawad Gita, it is said, "How can you attain *yoga*, when you have not dropped *sankalpas* (i.e. desires, intentions and plans)? How can one smile?

The first thing to do is to expand desire. The second thing is to see the futility of the fulfilment of the desire, and the third, is to see that, if it's fulfilled – so what? You are left, where you were. Nothing big has happened. It has not done anything. It has not touched you.

You know, if you drive through villages, or small towns, you will see stray dogs on the roads, and since cars aren't seen in these parts much, do you know what happens, when you drive your car in any of these places?

The stray dog in the street will run with the car because till then, it had been the fastest running animal in that village or town! But now, there's this car that is "running"... and the dog thinks, "What is this thing that is running?" So, the dog overtakes the car... and after overtaking the car, it looks very stupid, because it doesn't know what to do next! It put its hundred percent into overtaking the car – and then it doesn't know what to do! It barks all the way, overtakes the car... and then just stands there, looking stupid! It's a sight to see! Have you not noticed this ever?

We get desires fulfilled – so what? *Then* what? We achieve desires... to look stupid!

Say, all that a person wishes for, is to become the President of India, or rather, the Prime Minister of India. For twenty-five years, a person struggles to become the Prime Minister... and after becoming the Prime Minister, he (or she) says, "Oh! I struggled for this?! I had a very peaceful life... There's no charm in this..." – *You* could realize this *now*.

All your life, you try to become a famous actor: "I *want* to become a famous actor..." Once you become famous, are you happy? No! You are more miserable!

I am *not* saying that one should not have desires, or that all desires are stupid. I'm saying that thinking the fulfilment of desires will bring you something, or take you somewhere, is an illusion. Do you get what I mean? Have desire – and let it be fulfilled, but *don't anchor* your life in it. It will prove to be an illusion. It's a very delicate, fine balance. But, what do we do? We either have a pessimistic attitude or a feverish one!

THE ART OF LIVING

In the first case, we say, "You should *never* desire at all!" This is being pessimistic in life: "Oh! What is life! I am going to die, anyway... so let's eat, whatever I have to eat, let's eat whatever I have to fill my stomach!"

In the second case, we say, "Oh! *I want* this thing to be fulfilled! Oh! *I want* that thing to happen! Oh! *I want* so many millions!" Your whole mind is full of millions and millions – your whole mind is full of feverishness –feverishness of desire.
So when a desire arises, find a balance.

Do you get this?

I tell you, those, who take it easy, when it comes to desire, are not lazy – they are being active about it! Whether you are feverish about something, or pessimistic about it, life will not "move it".

So be on the golden middle path!

MEDITATION & PRANAYAMA

Let us go over some *Yoga Sutras...*

How does one sit for meditation?
– *Sukhsthirma* (comfortably and steady)!

What is the definition of *"asana"*?

"Asana" means, a steady and comfortable posture. So whatever you do, sit steady. Whenever you sit for meditation, just see if you are steady and if you are comfortable. Simply putting your attention ("I am now sitting very steady and very comfortably...") is good enough – Meditation will start happening! Are you getting what I am saying?

Sit comfortably... and *know* that you are sitting comfortably and steady. See, you sit in any posture – but you may still feel a little twitchy! Don't try to bring too much comfort to yourself! Your effort to bring comfort creates discomfort! That is why, the *sutra* didn't simply say, "be comfortable" – It says, "Be steady and comfortable." Both, steadiness and being comfortable, are very important.

The next step is: *"Prayatna Shaithalyath Anantha Samapathi."*

This *sutra* is so beautiful! It says, "Let go of the effort." Your *effort* to correct something, to have something, to repair something, to achieve something – all this is *effort*. You are sitting, having let effort loose... and there is some tension, or something, in the mind, in the body, or elsewhere. Now don't *try* to get rid of this. The next step is letting go of the effort: "*Prayatna Shaithalyath Anantha Samapathi*".

Becoming infinity – This is "*asana*"… and the effect is "*Dwandhwa Nabhighatha*", which means duality and the resolution of conflict (i.e. conflicts get resolved). So, unless you have *asana siddhi*, there is no further progress.

This is called perfection in *asana* – to be able to sit… and dissolve into infinity. So when you start with this in one posture, in another posture, and in yet another posture, and so on, then, no matter what you do, the whole set of *asanas*, will be meditative.

Pranayama "comes" in this state of *asanas*.

What is *"pranayama"*?

Pranayama is *breaking* the rhythm of the *prana* that is "going" in and out of our systems. Are you getting this?

If you break the flow, the *natural* flow (whatever it is) of *prana* – that is *pranayama* – because what *appears* to be natural, is really *not* natural – in fact, it is unnatural; only, it has become sort of second nature to us, and that is why, we *think* it is natural. So, in that state, when you sit and observe the breath… and then change its mode – *pranayama* happens.

Don't do this as and when, or however, you like! That's why a particular "ratio" is kept (or taught) – Be with this ratio; it is the perfect one.

When you sit in meditation, what are the things that can bother you?

These "things" are called "*vikaras*".

So, what can bother you?

Lust can bother you. The first thing that could come into your mind is lust. Greed can bother you. The third thing that could bother you is anger towards somebody. Jealousy can bother you. Entanglement or attachment, to somebody or something, can bother you. So, it's these four or five things that bother you.

Arrogance cannot bother you in meditation, because for arrogance, you need another person, you need somebody else. When you are sitting alone in meditation, arrogance doesn't play a part. Jealousy can be combated, when you stop comparing. Don't compare yourself to anybody. You *know* all this, but still, when these *vikaras* arise or "happen", then *asanas* help.

Another thing we can do is "*pratyahara*". "*Pratyahara*" means, saying, "Okay... *This* moment, I *don't* want to see anything in the world. Right *this* moment, I *don't* want to smell anything. Right *this* moment, I *don't* care for any taste – whether it's ice-cream, french-fries, or anything else; even the most tastiest thing – I *don't* care for it, right this moment. I don't care for any sensation of touch, this moment. This moment, I don't care for any beautiful sound."

In this manner, we retrieve our mind back from all the five senses... and bring it to itself.

"This moment, I don't want..." Are you getting what I am saying? This moment. Then, release from the clutches of the "*maya*" (illusion) of the world, happens immediately. This is because *maya* is such that it drags your mind outwards and outwards all the time. So meditation happens, when one retrieves the mind back... and we do this through techniques.

Remember just *one* thing about *asanas*: Be steady and comfortable. Ask yourself, "Am I steady right now? Am I comfortable?" Then let go into infinity... That's it. Any duality and restlessness are dissolved immediately.

This is all you need to have — That's why this is called a *sutra*. Just remember this *sutra*... and sit. The sitting itself can elevate you — take you a very long way. Do this, when you meditate... and see how it feels at various different times — comfortable and steady... relaxed... dissolving into infinity.

MEDITATION AND PRAYER

Prayer means asking – "I want that, I want this..." – or expressing gratitude for whatever has been given... Prayer means saying something.

Meditation means listening – "What are you going to say? I am willing to listen..." If you can say this, then *that* is meditation.

Prayer means requests, or urging. Therefore, *before* you pray, you *must* meditate. You should meditate, even *after* you pray.

In all our scriptures, as part of our ancient tradition, there is a "*dhyana shloka*" (a *mantra* or chant for meditation).

Previously, there was nothing in place of this *mantra*. "They" would say, "*Dhyana*" (meditation)… and give a break. However, people did not understand the significance of this break (during which, they were supposed to meditate). They thought, "Why this break? After saying 'meditation', it has been left incomplete… How come there is nothing here? Let us add a *shloka* (chant) in Sanskrit with four-five lines… and fill up the blank."

So they inserted a *shloka*, instead of doing a meditation… and this is now known as the *dhyana shloka*.

THE ART OF LIVING

So, what is happening, now?

In the name of meditation, *shlokas* are uttered rapidly and then, one proceeds. They do not even meditate now-a-days!

There is also mention of the *pranayams* in our ancient scriptures. They say that before conducting a thread ceremony, a wedding ceremony, or any auspicious ceremony, the *pranayam has* to be done – but, what is being done now?

One just holds one's nose, touches one's ears... and finishes the formality. Before performing the *sankalpa* (The *sankalpa* is the "intention *mantra*", which is recited before performing a *pooja* – whatever you desire, and the *pooja*, which you are going to perform in order to obtain divine blessings for the fulfilment of that desire, are all mentioned in the *sankalpa*), people just hold their noses, and finish off the formality! Nobody has explained the proper procedure involved in "doing" a *sankalpa*.

When you go to a temple, a plate with flowers in it, is brought to you... and the priest asks you to touch that plate.

Then the priest tells you to pray – declare your *sankalpa* or intention. Your name, your birth star and *gotra* (the "class" into which, you were born) are also mentioned.

After this, the *mantra* that is chanted is:

"Shubhe shobhane muhurte
[in this auspicious moment...]

day brahmanaha
[this very creation of Brahma...]

witeya parardhe
[afternoon time...]

Shri shweta varaha kalpe
[this *kalpa*, in which we are all living – known as
"shri shweta varadha"...]

vaivavata manvantare
[this age of Vaisvata Manu...]

kaliyuge prathana pade
[in the first *pada* of *kaliyuga*...]

bharata varshe bharata khande
jambodwepe dandakaranye
godavayaha dakshine tere
shalivahana shake bouddhavatare
shre rama kshetre chandramanesa
prabhavadi shashti samvatsaranam madhye
[among the 60 *samvatsaras* (years)... (As per the Hindu calendar, every 60 years constitute one cycle, and every year in the 60 years has a name) – "*samvatsarasya*" (during the *pooja*, the name of the running year is mentioned)

a yane
[*uttarayana* or *dakshinayana* – i.e. depending on the position of the sun, the movement towards the equinox in the northern direction (*uttarayana*) in the first 6 months of the year, or in the southern direction (*dakshinayana*) in the second 6 months of the year, is mentioned]

rutau
[the *rutu* – or the season of the year, is mentioned]

mase
[the name of the running month, i.e. *masa*, is mentioned]

pakshe
[*paksha* is the moon status – whether it is a full moon *(shukla paksa)* or a new moon *(Krishna paksha)* during the *pooja*]

tithaee
[that day...]

vasare
[the name of the week...]

nakshatre
[the star of that day…]

evangua vistreshana vishistayam shubha tithau poojam karishye"
[Today, I perform the *pooja*, which is all of the above mentioned…]

Our mind is expanded to the time, when the Universe was created… and when was that?

"This creation was born four crore and many thousands of years ago. The creation is remembered, since its inception to the present day. After this, the time of Brahma is mentioned – It is *dwiteya paradha* (i.e. it is now the afternoon period of Brahma). In this afternoon period of Brahma, in this *kalpa**, known as *shweta varaha*, in this *vaivasvata mavantara***, in this *kaliyuga****, in the first *pada***** of *kaliyuga*, in this vast creation, which has crores of planets, in this small planet, called earth, in this Indian continent, in the Indian peninsula to the south of the Godavari river (*Godavaryaha dakshine tere*), in the era of *shalinivahana*, in this period, following the *avataar* of Buddha (*Bouddhavatare*), in the land of Rama (*Rama kshetre*), in such and such a year, in this *ayana*, in this season, on this day, in this time, in this place, I am doing this, in this…"

---

*   Four yugas constitute one kalpa

**   Manu or the "first father" of this period is know as vaivasvata

***   There are four yugas – Satyayuga, Tretayuga, Dwaparayuga and Kaliyuga. The yuga that is running now is known as Kaliyuga

****   There are four padas, or parts, to every yuga. The time span of kaliyuga is 25,000 years. The first pada has been completed now, i.e. the life span of the first pada is now over – the first 5,000 years have passed now.

In this manner, the mind that is "expanded to the macrocosm" is brought to a focus, is brought to the microcosmic level.

Then, one says, "Let good 'happen to' everybody. Let everybody be prosperous… and for this purpose, I am going to perform this worship" – and the *sankalpa* is completed.

What are the activities usually performed by us?

We usually keep doing those activities, which our small mind wants us to do. The small mind feels, "Today, I want to eat jackfruit," and so you go and eat jackfruit. The small mind feels it should eat ice-cream… and so you eat ice-cream. We spend all our lives, trying to constantly satisfy the small mind.

It is important to perform some activity, which makes the big mind happy. That is why we say "*parameshwara preetyartham*" (i.e. for the sake of making the Divine happy, I do this work"), and the intention or *sankalpa* is made in the present moment.

What were you told to do, before performing the *sankalpa*?

You were asked to drink a little water – "*achamaniyam samarpayami*" – and adjust your throat; do *pranayama*. That is why a little water is drunk before the *pranayama*. However, have you seen how *pranayama* is done, now-a-days?

They just hold their noses and let go! There is a proverb in Kannada, which says, "Will your work get done, if you sit holding your nose?" What is actually meant is that before you perform any activity, hold your nose *properly* (i.e. perform *pranayama* properly). They knew that by performing *pranayama* in the right manner, all your activities would succeed – would happen well. This is known as "the art of *sankalpa*".

We should *expand* the consciousness in this manner. The more our minds expand, the more capability we acquire to do greater work – All our work gets done *faster* and in an *easy* manner! The small mind is always caught up in (or with) troubles and it is always irritated. That is why it is important to expand our minds. This is known as *sankalpa*. It is said that *sankalpa* "happens" during meditation.

Our lives progress because of *sankalpa*, but with these *sankalpas*, *vikalpas* (or mal-intentions) also arise. If you decide, "I want to do this…" then, simultaneously, a *vikalpa* arises: "Oh! If I do this, then that will *not* happen. This is *not* possible! I do *not* know whether it is possible for me to do so…" When such thoughts arise, the power of the *sankalpa* (or the intention) decreases.

The removal of all *vikalpas* is only possible through the path of love and devotion. When you surrender you mal-intentions through devotion, and when you pray, *everything* vanishes – You are freed… and then, the *sankalpa* continues…

YOUR QUESTIONS, ANSWERED...

Q: You have told us a lot about meditation, but I would like to know more, please.

Meditation is *not* trying to think of something. Meditation is relaxing deeply. If you are concentrating on a problem, then you are not relaxing. So what do we do?

We just let go...

Meditation is almost like sleep, but it's not sleep. It is what happens right after the *Sudarshan Kriya* – When you are lying down, what's in your mind?
Nothing! There is nothing – it's blank. *That* is

meditation. Or, when you are really happy, when you are resting, then, what is the state of your mind?

That is a meditative mind.

Even, when you are in deep love... and you are reposing in love, then *that* is meditation.
It's very simple! When the mind becomes free from agitation, when it becomes calm and serene, and is at peace, then, meditation happens.

By meditating, you can turn your body into a powerhouse as you generate an inner source of energy.

Q: When I begin reading or writing, my mind moves on to other subjects. Please suggest how I can concentrate, and reach or achieve my goals?

Energy comes to us primarily through three sources – one is food, the other is sleep and the third is breath. You all know that when you lack energy, you must eat, or that when you lack energy, you must sleep, but you don't know – or atleast you pretend to not know – that you also have to breathe properly in order to be energetic. So if you learn the *Pranayama* and practice the *Sudarshan Kriya* (i.e. do some breathing), it can change your energy levels. Meditation is thus also a source of energy.

Now, when you "change your energy", your mind is calm, and it can concentrate more. Concentration is a by-product of meditation.

Meditation is really de-concentration; letting go, but we have the wrong notion that meditation is concentration. It is not so – it is actually the *opposite* of concentration!

To do any job, one needs concentration, but to meditate, one doesn't need concentration. Anybody can meditate… and after one meditates, what comes out is alertness, and a focussed mind.

Meditation calms the mind. It feels good.

In our daily lives, we have to handle paying bills, parking vehicles, and other mundane things. Now, how can we do this, with the same calm mind – i.e.

without getting irritated or perturbed?

You take a shower in the morning to clean your body, right? After that, you do all your daily activities, don't you? You don't have to keep taking a shower throughout the day! It is like that. You meditate and calm your mind – Then, go on with your other activities.

It is not easy to keep yourself undisturbed, but it *will* happen as you keep doing the practice (i.e. the *Sudarshan Kriya*, the *Pranayama*…), regularly. Then it becomes easy.

Q: How can I keep the mind quiet?

You want the answer?
[The person says, "Yes!"]
What's happening? …What's happening?
[The person says, "I'm feeling quiet…"]
Got it?!
When you are waiting for something, you become quiet… If you extend this, it will lead you to meditation… or frustration!

Q: Why is meditation so boring for me?

In the beginning, it may be boring, but that will *change*. Stay with it! Go step-by-step. Meditation is *resting in yourself.* Meditation is becoming the seer, from being the seen.

Q: Why do old memories bother me, when I sit for meditation?

It does not matter! Don't lose heart! Let them come! Say, "Come, sit with me, five-year-old, or ten-year-old, or twenty-year-old memories. Come! Sit with me."

The more you want to run away from them, the more they will bother you.

Q: I have no time for yoga and meditation. What can I do?

Yoga and meditation *give* you time! No time for these, means – you have to go to a hospital, or a doctor!

Q: What are the benefits of meditation?

There are plenty of benefits! Your health problems stop (for e.g. you don't "get" blood pressure), you experience mental peace and greater happiness, your mind becomes clear, your intuition develops and negative influences, due to planetary positions and various obstacles, are removed – problems "become small", before "they come" to you... There are plenty of other benefits too!

Q: Can meditation remove bad karma?

Yes.

Q: Is there any maximum limit to how much we can meditate?

Just do as much as is necessary. Only do as much as is necessary. There is no need to do too much. Meditation is like taking a bath. You need meditation to wash the mind, and once the mind is clean, it is okay.

Q: You are constantly working for us – so, how much time do You get for sadhana (the practice)?

The whole time!

Q: Could You please elaborate more on what obstructs meditation?

There are four things that obstruct you from having a calm, serene, meditative mind.

What are these four things?

The first, is the desire to do something; some desire to do something – It could be a simple thing – like washing clothes, or going to get an air-ticket, or planning: "What will I do? Maybe, in the next few years, the coming years, I will…" It could be any planning. Maybe you sit and plan, "Oh! Which building should come where? …And how should I 'do' the garden?"

This desire, or planning, in the mind, about business – about anything – will sit like a rock in your mind. When you sit to meditate, you will feel there is a rock in your head. How many of you have felt like this? Many of you have felt this – like there is something – some obstacle. This is "*ichha*". *Ichha* means desire… and it has the same "quality", as when you hate somebody.

When you feel hatred ("*dwesh*") – when you hate somebody, then too, you feel like a rock has been put on your head. Have you experienced this? How many of you have experienced this?

"*Ichha*", "*dwesh*", "*sukh*", "*dukh*" – These are the four things that bring this sort of inertia into your brain cells.

Sukh means too much excitement; "a big" happiness – then too, you feel unsettled. The same thing happens, when there is sorrow – when there is great sorrow...

See, the first two (*ichha* and *dwesh*) "sit" like rocks, while the other two (*sukh* and *dukh*) are like steam. So desire, or planning (to do something), and hatred, are like rocks – heavy. *Sukh* and *dukh*, however, don't "sit" like rocks. In both, *sukh* (pleasure) and *dukh* (pain), the sensation is like steam – boiling, unsettled. It's like you are in a pressure cooker, and there's this big pressure from the steam.

These four things, or modes of consciousness, can obstruct you from being in a natural, lively state of mind. They obstruct your meditation.

Surrender means dropping all these four things!

When you have surrendered, there is no planning. I mean, you should plan, but it should be like your coat, or raincoat. When you go for a shower, you don't go with your raincoat on, or with your tie and suit on, or with your shoes on! The moment, you get into the shower, you take off all your clothes, don't you? Only then, can you *really* shower – only then, is there any meaning to showering!

In the same way, meditation has meaning, only when you can put aside your plans – and that is called surrender. Do you see what I am saying?

What does "surrender" mean?

It is "giving custody"! It's: "See, all my plans, my sorrows, my pleasures – everything, I now 'keep' here with the Divine… and now, I am free; I am relaxed." The moment freedom comes, relaxation comes, and meditation happens, "*samadhi*" happens, equanimity happens. Do you see that? Everybody has desires, everybody plans, but only a few have the ability to plan… and then take the coat off, and hang it on a hanger. Then again, whenever they want, they can take it. Otherwise, you are stuck with your raincoat… and you smell foul all the time.

Just imagine a situation, where somebody is sweating a lot in the hot summer, but he (or she) stands underneath a shower, with his (or her) raincoat on – then, any amount of showering is not going to take the foul smell out of them.

Similarly, you may be meditating for thirty or forty years, but if you do not know, how to take your coat off again and again, then, you land up in the same place.

I have talked about this in the *Bhakti Sutras...*

Understand these four principles – It is very important. I will repeat them again, so that you don't forget:

Ichha, dwesh, sukh and *dukh* – these four are the basis of any *sankalpa*. So, unless you know how to take these coats off, you can never practice *yoga*.
Ichha means desire. I am *not* saying that desire is bad, or that you should not desire – I am saying, you should be able to *let go*; be able to say, "So what?!" If you have had a great desire (whatever it is)...

and it "happened" – Then, what?

Dwesh means hatred.

Sukh means pleasure, excitement, or craving for excitement, and *dukh* means sadness, or sorrow. Examine all sorrow… You will see that the cause behind any sorrow is – "Me" or "mine". The moment you see: "Oh! What is mine?!" – then, the steam, the pressure, the pressure cooker's pressure, gets a little less…

Anyway, time heals you. You cannot have the same degree of any of the four, over a long period. That's why, notice what is happening with you. Many a time, you feel the rock. You don't know what is happening, or how to get rid of it, and then you just worry…

After a couple of days, or weeks, it disappears, or becomes lesser and lesser. I've already spoken about this. See, just lie there – Be present, alert, awake and wait...

Don't be anxious to feel love. Many, *try* to feel love, when it is not coming up! This is another problem! You have felt great love; you have felt waves of great love and bliss at some time. So, at other times, when they are not there, you feel bad, and you want to "get" them back – you try to get back to that; you try to hold on to that. But, all this doer-ship or effort becomes counter-productive. Do you see that?
Just be. Just be... and wait. Then, it happens again...

Q: How does one examine a desire?

Where are you, when a desire arises... and where are you, after the desire is fulfilled?

You will find it is like being on a merry-go-round! You get down at the same place, where you got on, the first time! You know, in a merry-go-round, you get on at some place... and it goes round and round and round... and in the end, you come back to the same place!

Similarly, you find that even if a desire is fulfilled, you are the same, even though you have been running around the whole time! If the desire is fulfilled, you are at the same place. If the desire is not fulfilled, then too, you are at the same place. If the desire is not fulfilled, it leaves you with a little more tension and stiffness in your nervous system.

See, a Master says things at different times to suit different ages, to suit different situations, to suit different people. So, you all have to look in to these aspects. All the Masters have (or had) a purpose, a time, a place and a group. If people are told, "You don't need to desire. It's fine. You eat, drink and sleep – that is enough." – then, these people would not even meditate. They would not even start enquiring about life, about Truth.

So the instruction then is: "If you are going to desire, desire for the *highest*, desire for something *more* in life." With this, you are *on* the path, but once you are on the path – once you have driven back home, and once your car has been shut off – now, I tell you, "Get out of the car!"

Instructions are different at different places – otherwise, you will sit, dozing off, in your car, in your garage, for all time to come! I am telling you, "Here is a beautiful bed! Come! Get out of the car. You are at home! Sleep well. Rest well."

Let go of all these things that you are doing. Let go of desires.

Q: In meditation, what is the significance of "waiting"?

What happens in your mind, when you have to wait?

What is happening in your mind, right now?
Do you see time passing by?
This very waiting can take you into meditation. When you have to wait, you can either be frustrated, or meditative. Meditation is "feeling the time"...
Can you observe every moment that is passing by right now?

Q: I am unable to meditate. Please explain.

When you are mad or angry, you say, "I don't know. Don't ask me."
Even when you're asked, "What's your name?" – the answer is, "I don't know."
Even if you're asked, "Where are you going?" – the reply is, "I don't know. Don't ask me anything."

When you are mad, you say, "I don't know." This is an ugly "I don't know." Your whole journey is from this ugly "I don't know," to a beautiful "I don't know!" This move... this patience to wait and be with what is – That is a gift in itself. Hmm?

So this life is a gift. Time is a gift. Breath is a gift. Meditation is a gift.
You don't bargain with gifts. You don't demand gifts. No exchange! No refunds!
Gifts come with a guarantee of course – a lifetime guarantee! However, when we don't understand that "this is a gift," that's when we really miss out. Meditation is such a gift...

The more we serve, the deeper we are able to go into meditation. You cannot go deeper into meditation just by understanding, reading and listening. You have to have the heart to serve – then, it happens.

Also, there's a time... See, many come here and listen; but when it's not time, they are really unable to do anything! They are unable to meditate, they're unable to do the Sudarshan Kriya or even the course; but they come back after 7, 8, 9, 10 years – some even after 12 - 13 years.

So time is a gift. Meditation is a gift. Don't demand a gift, but know you are worthy to be given a gift! You know, there are two positions:

Either you think you are too worthy and you start demanding – then the gift doesn't come to you; or you feel you are not worthy of the gift at all. Then, even though the gift is right in front of you, you are not able to "own" it!

Feel that it belongs to you. The middle path is what is needed – neither demand nor feel unworthy.

Q: I always go to the sleep while meditating! How do I solve this? Does this happen to everybody? What experiences do others have?

Don't worry about other people's experiences! Be with your own experience... This experience varies from time to time. So don't worry! It's okay!

Q: What is the difference between meditation and sleep?

One is vertical and the other is horizontal! For now,

just think of them like this. However, when you sit for meditation tomorrow, don't think about this, for then, you'll neither be able to meditate, nor sleep!

Q: Sometimes one feels a sense of barrenness – a loss of joy. Is this just a phase? Does the innocence, the spontaneous joyfulness return?

Of course!
Sometimes, you will feel sadness and sometimes, other feelings may also come up, but they just pass by. Put more attention on the breath and on the sensations in the body... Every emotion has a corresponding sensation in the body, and that sensation, in turn, creates that very same emotion. Do you understand, what I am saying?

An event created an emotion inside you, and the emotion creates a similar type of atmosphere around you again... and this cycle goes on. The only way to break this cycle is to observe a sensation as a sensation – to de-link it from emotions. It is simple – very simple. If you meditate for just a little while, you will understand that. It's clearer on an experiential level.

Q: I can only meditate> when You conduct a meditation> live – otherwise I can't! What do I do?

There is nothing like *dead* meditation! *Just meditate!*

Q: My beloved Guruji, I think I could be dispassionate about everything, but You! How could I ever be dispassionate about You!

A scattered mind can have a focus! If the mind is too scattered, when it "comes to a focus", then, the next job will be done by nature, automatically! It will happen... and it will happen naturally – this is already happening – Isn't it? The mind withdraws from all these experiences...

You cannot separate the body and the mind. The gross aspect of the mind is the body, and the subtle aspect of the body is the mind. So they withdraw and rest, simultaneously.

They go into a state of inertia, wherein the knowledge in the mind, in the consciousness, goes to the background – just like what happens as the sun sets. What happens then?

Night "comes"... but the sun has not disappeared; it's "hiding". In the same way, when the knowledge, the awareness in this life, the consciousness, withdraw and go into another dimension, then, one is overtaken by sleep. That's why it is called *"tamo guna tamasik"*(the dark) – Inertia takes over... It has its time... and then wakefulness comes again.

The best comparison of our three states of consciousness (waking, sleeping and dreaming) is with nature. Nature sleeps, awakes and dreams! These happen on a magnificent scale in existence... and these are also

happening in the human body, on a different scale. Wakefulness and sleep are like sunrise and darkness, while dreams are like the twilight in-between.
Meditation is like the flight to outer space, where there is no sunset, no sunrise – nothing!

Q: While working, we need to think intensely, and while meditating, we need to observe thoughts. How can we balance this?

When you are tired of chasing thoughts – meditate!

Q: How can I be assured of salvation and a perfect life on this planet?

You need a warranty on the spiritual path too, don't you?!

Examine, how much time you spend on this path...

Evaluate the *seva* (service) you are doing... How much are you meditating?

There should be a balance between *seva* and meditation. Those, who do a lot of *seva*, get burnt out, if they don't make time for meditation, and those, who only meditate, it becomes "dry", if they don't make time for *seva*. So, you need both – *seva* and meditation.

Q: What is the best way to reach bliss?

What is the *best* way? – One, is by meditating, and the other, is by serving the people around you – by getting into some service activity.

You know the technique to getting depressed is to sit and only think: "What about me? What about me?" – all the time! That's good enough to get thoroughly depressed!

Seeing God, within you, is meditation. Seeing God, in the people around you, is love or service. They go hand-in-hand.

THE ART OF LIVING
&
THE INTERNATIONAL ASSOCIATION FOR HUMAN VALUES

Transforming Lives

THE FOUNDER

H. H. SRI SRI RAVI SHANKAR

Feted the world over by governments and the common man alike, His Holiness Sri Sri Ravi Shankar has been instrumental in enabling millions from every walk of life, lead lives that are happier, fuller, healthier and stress-free. Founder of the Art of Living, spread across 146 countries today and the International Association for Human Values, headquartered in Geneva, His Holiness, through His organisations, revives human values, promotes global peace and guides comprehensive service and development endeavours that transform lives all over the globe.

In a world fraught with conflict, His message that all individuals, societies, civilizations, cultures, religions and spiritual traditions share common human values has deeply resonated everywhere, with a power and gentleness that are uniquely exuded by H. H. Sri Sri Ravi Shankar Himself. He inspires sustained individual commitment to joyful living, selfless service and self-awareness through His eternal message of peace, love and *seva* (service), addressing diverse audiences, including Heads of State, the United Nations, the World Economic Forum, scientists, legislators and various parliaments, political and business leaders, academic and social institutions, other decision-makers etc. The innumerable awards and honours conferred upon His Holiness reflect the depth and extent of the gratitude felt for his inspiration, wisdom and presence.

Yet, beyond all these immense, visible, tangible achievements, He is a *Guru* whose touch is personal. He has always maintained that we are here to develop the individual, not a movement. He lights the flame of love in one heart, this one heart transforms another ten and these in turn transform another hundred. This is how He works, creating opportunities for leadership and service to every single person connected with him. His compassion, joy, love, wisdom and playfulness have given a whole new dimension to spirituality.

Born on May 13th 1956, in Papanasam (Tamil Nadu, India), His Holiness Sri Sri Ravi Shankar was often found rapt in meditation as a little boy. By the time He was four, He was already reciting the *Bhagwad Gita* and other scriptures. As a young boy, He would often tell His friends, "People all over the world are waiting for me." By age seventeen, He had completed His education in both Vedic literature and modern science.

In 1982, H. H. Sri Sri Ravi Shankar began teaching the *Sudarshan Kriya*, a powerful, yet simple breathing technique that eliminates stress and brings one into the present moment completely. This is taught around the world as a part of the Art of Living Programmes, benefiting and healing numerous people in various ways.

THE ART OF LIVING

IN SERVICE AROUND
THE WORLD

The largest volunteer-based network in the world, with a wide range of social, cultural and spiritual activities, the Art of Living has reached out to **over 20 million people** from all walks of life, since 1982. A non-profit, educational, humanitarian organization, it is committed to creating peace from the level of the individual upwards, and fostering human values within the global community. Currently, the Art of Living service projects and educational programmes are carried out in **over 146 countries**. The organisation works in special consultative status with the Economic and Social Council of the United Nations, participating in a variety of committees and activities, related to health and conflict resolution.

THE ART OF LIVING STRESS ELIMINATION PROGRAMMES

HOLISTIC DEVELOPMENT OF BODY, MIND & SPIRIT

The Art of Living programmes are a combination of the best of ancient wisdom and modern science. They cater to every age group – children, youth, adults, and every section of society – rural communities, governments, corporate houses, etc. Emphasizing holistic living and personal self-development, the programmes facilitate the complete blossoming of an individual's full potential.

The cornerstone of all our workshops is the *Sudarshan Kriya*, a unique, potent breathing practice.

The Art of Living Course - Part I

The Art of Living Course - Part I is a simple, yet profound programme that offers the *Sudarshan Kriya*, practical spiritual knowledge, deep meditation and interactive processes. *The Sudarshan Kriya*, a unique breathing practice, formulated by His Holiness Sri Sri Ravi Shankar, is the cornerstone of all Art of Living Programmes. It is a powerful energiser that cleanses deep-rooted physical, mental and emotional stresses and toxins, thereby helping to synchronise the mind and body with the rhythms of nature. Serenity, centredness, better health, more harmonious relationships, greater joy and enthusiasm for life and are just some of the benefits of this course.

The Art of Living Course - Part II

The Art of Living Course - Part II takes one deeper into one's self. Very often, one takes a vacation, only to come back feeling more exhausted and in the need of another one! The Part II course is a vacation, in the true sense of the word, leaving one rejuvenated and relaxed, both physically and mentally. It includes *Sadhana* (spiritual practices), *Satsang* (spiritual communion through singing), *Seva* (service) and Silence.

Sahaj Samadhi Meditation

The *Sahaj Samadhi* Meditation is a delightfully simple, yet powerful process that allows one to experience the depth of the Being. Through this ancient, natural, graceful system of meditation the mind settles down, lets go off all stress and tension, and centres itself in the present moment, enabling one to experience profound silence and inner bliss.

Divya Samaaj ka Nirmaan (DSN)

A society is a reflection of its individuals, and the DSN empowers an individual to contribute positively to his (or her) society. *Divya Samaaj ka Nirmaan* (DSN) literally means "Creating a divine society". If you've ever asked yourself, "What can I do to make this world a better place?" – then, the DSN is your answer.

The All Round Training in Excellence (ART Excel)
(for 8-14 year olds)

Tailor-made for our young ones, The ART Excel is a highly effective programme that inspires and positively shapes the lives of children. It helps them release stress and overcome emotions like fear, anger, aggression, shyness etc., through the breath. It develops concentration, builds confidence and inculcates human values, such as sharing, caring, acceptance, trust and respect, through interactive games and various processes.

The Youth Empowerment Seminar (YES)
(for 15-21 year olds)

In an age where young adults grapple with peer pressure and stiff academic competition, the YES enables youth to excel by equipping them to handle their minds and emotions, inculcating a sense of belonging and instilling leadership skills. Through the *Sudarshan Kriya*, interactive processes, discussions and games, students benefit from improved memory, concentration, clarity, creativity and confidence.

The Prison Programme

The Prison Programme addresses the needs of prison inmates, as well as those individuals and institutions that combat crime and violence. The techniques taught, release stress, and help reduce violent tendencies and drug dependencies. The life skills, imparted in the Programme, also enable inmates accept responsibility for their past actions, and handle future conflict or stressful situations, successfully. The aim is to facilitate genuine rehabilitation so that inmates are truly able to make a fresh, new, happy beginning.

The Corporate Executive Programme (CEP)

The Corporate Executive Programme, also called the APEX (Achieving Personal Excellence) Programme, is highly specialized, practical and effective. It presents a paradigm shift, from "working hard" to "working smart" and provides employees with the solution to striking a balance between meeting the demands of one's personal life and professional commitments. It strengthens managers and employees, enabling them to experience unshakable calm and inner clarity in the face of any business challenge or crisis. In the corporate world, only the fittest survive and the CEP ensures true fitness at every level.

❋ ❋ ❋

THE INTERNATIONAL ASSOCIATION FOR HUMAN VALUES (IAHV)

The International Association for Human Values (IAHV) was founded in Geneva in 1997, to foster, on a global scale, a deeper understanding of the values that unite us as a single human community. Its vision is to celebrate distinct traditions and diversity, while simultaneously creating a greater understanding and appreciation of our many shared principles. To this end, the IAHV develops and promotes programmes that generate awareness and encourage the practice of human values in everyday life. It upholds that the incorporation of human values into all aspects of life, will ultimately lead to harmony amidst diversity, and the development of a more peaceful, just and sustainable world. The IAHV works in collaboration with partners dedicated to similar goals, including governments, multilateral agencies, educational institutions, NGOs, corporations and individuals.

THE ART OF LIVING

Service Projects

Sustainable Rural Development

With the objective of social and economic reliance, both, at the individual and community level, this Art of Living Programme works at holistically strengthening and empowering communities worldwide, at the grassroots level, by addressing the needs of the rural communities' poor and disadvantaged. It achieves this through a variety of programmes, like the Sri Sri Rural Development Programme (SSRDP), the Youth Leadership Training Programme (YLTP) and the 5H Programme (where the 5Hs are Health, Hygiene, Homes, Human Values and Harmony amidst diversity). Hundreds of thousands, the world over, have benefited from these Programmes.

Organic Farming

The Art of Living is taking concrete, substantial steps to revive traditional, efficient agricultural practices like organic (chemical-free) farming, which consequently bring joy and prosperity to the farming community. It also runs the Sri Sri Mobile Agricultural Institute (SSMAI), which brings agriculture-related knowledge, right to the farmers' doorsteps, providing and instilling self-confidence.

Trauma Relief

From an earthquake in Iran, to a tsunami in Sri Lanka, from floods in Germany, to cyclones in India, from wars in Iraq and Croatia, to a school-massacre in Russia, from strife in Bosnia, and Afghanistan, to 9/11 in the USA, over the years, whenever tragedy has struck our planet, Art of Living volunteers, the world over, have come together to answer the cry for help in a unanimous spirit of service and solidarity, irrespective of caste, creed, religion, or geography.

Peace Initiatives

In a world feeding off intolerance, insecurity, doubt, and conflict, His Holiness Sri Sri Ravi Shankar, leads the way in extending invitations of friendship and peace. His unrelenting commitment to build bridges between estranged communities, and to help people overcome the trauma of conflict, pave the way to mutual trust and lasting peace. The Art of Living has been working to promote friendly ties within and between several regions, including Afghanistan, Kosovo, Pakistan, Israel, Lebanon, Nepal and Kashmir (India), with the aim of peace, and rapid economic development.

Education

The Art of Living is committed to making free-of-cost, quality education accessible to the poor, providing a joyful and inspiring learning environment to children from urban, rural and tribal areas. A range of schools, offering value-based education, have been set up: Tribal Schools, Rural Schools, Sri Sri Seva Mandirs (for children from slum, or urban low-income, areas), the Ashram School (catering to first generation learners from the villages surrounding the Bangalore International Centre), Vedic/ Agama Schools (reviving traditional Vedic knowledge), and Sri Sri Ravi Shankar Vidya Mandirs (catering to higher income groups). The organisation also runs institutions of higher education.

Women Empowerment

The Art of Living runs Programmes aimed at uplifting women in the poorest villages of the rural world. The mission is to transform the lives of women and girls, who are illiterate, emotionally abused, and often afflicted with serious health problems. The organisation imparts basic literacy skills and vocational training, facilitating self-sufficiency. In addition, they are made aware about hygiene, and taught yoga and meditation. The increase in their self-respect and dignity is immeasurable. One such programme running in Urugalli (a village in Karnataka, India) is VISTA (Value Integrated Services to All), India.

Rehabilitation of Drug Addicts

Through its programmes, the Art of Living has been working with victims of drug abuse, both on its own, and in partnership with other organizations. The aim is to aid drug-addicts completely overcome their drug dependencies, thus facilitating true rehabilitation.

INTERNATIONAL CENTRES

INDIA
21st km, Kanakapura Road
Udayapura
Bangalore - 560 062
Karnataka
Telephone: 0091 80-30622473
Fax: 0091 80-28432832
Email: vvkpress@gmail.com

CANADA
Box 170-13 Infinity Road
St. Mathieu-du-Parc
Quebec, G0X 1N0
Telephone: 001 819-532-3328
Fax: 001 819-532-2033
Email: artofliving.northeast@sympatico.ca

GERMANY
Bad Antogast 1
77728 Oppenau
Telephone: 0049 7804-910 923
Fax: 0049 7804-910 924
Email: info@artofliving.de

THE ART OF LIVING

❀❀❀

- www.srisriravishankar.org •
  • www.artofliving.org •

  • www.iahv.org •
  • www.5h.org •

  • www.srisrischools.net •

❀❀❀